The Emperor's Kingdom

PENGUINS ON ICE

Dr. Roger Kirkwood

wild dog

This edition published in 2010 by

wild dog books

5 Gertrude Street
Fitzroy Vic 3065
Australia
61 + 3 + 9419 9406
61 + 3 + 9419 1214 (fax)
dog@bdb.com.au

wild dog books is an imprint of black dog books

Designed by Guy Holt Design
Printed and bound in China by Everbest Printing Pty Ltd

Distributed in the U.S.A. by
Scholastic Inc.
New York, NY 10012

Photo Credits: Bryan and Cherry Alexander/Hedgehog House, front cover; Corbis/Photolibrary, pii–iii; Roger Kirkwood, pp 2–3, 4–5, 7, 9, 12–13, 20–21, 22–23, 24, 25, 26; Auscape/Hedgehog House, pp 10–11; Armin Rose/ Shutterstock, pp 6–7, 25; Galen Rowell/Photolibrary, pp 8–9; Frederique Oliver/ Hedgehog House, pp 11, 12–13, 18; Frans Lanting/Corbis, pp 14–15, 16–17; Gentoo Multimedia/Shutterstock, pp 14, 16, 24, 26; Thorsten Milse/Photolibrary, pp 18–19; Colin Monteath / Hedgehog House, p 23, 24; Garry Yim/ Shutterstock, p27, Jason Cranberry, p26

ISBN: 9781742031583 (hbk)

0 9 8 7 6 5 4 3 2 1   10 11 12 13 14 15

Contents

Emperors of the Ice

Antarctica in winter is a very cold place.
So cold that the surface of the ocean freezes.

While most animals leave for warmer climates, one species comes ashore to breed.

This is the story of the Emperor Penguins.

February–April

In February and March, Emperor Penguins feed to build energy reserves for the breeding period. In April, they gather at colony sites on the sea-ice. Males and females come to these places and form pairs.

Each Emperor Penguin has a unique call. Mates learn their partner's call so they can find each other among the thousands of penguins at the colony.

May

Each female lays one large egg onto the ice then quickly scoops it onto her feet. She passes the egg to her mate, then heads out to the open sea.

June-July

After crossing up to fifty miles
of ice, the females find open water.
They feed during daylight hours.
In winter this far south, they have
just four hours of light each day.

June-July

Male Emperor Penguins are left at the colony, each balancing an egg on his feet to keep it warm. For the next two months they are devoted to their egg and will not feed.

A male Emperor Penguin will lose about half its body weight in the months that it cares for its egg. A fold of tummy skin rolls over the top of the egg to protect it from the wind and cold.

June–July

Males at the colony have to huddle together to keep warm. A penguin outside a huddle uses its energy reserves twice as quickly as a penguin inside a huddle.

When the wind is strong, the windchill is freezing. Males stream down the outside of the huddle, trying to get away from the wind.

Viewed from above, the huddle looks like a honeycomb of penguins.

August

At the end of winter, the eggs start to hatch. A chick's first meal will be a special milk from its dad's throat. Soon the well-fed females will march across the ice and back to their colony.

At the edge of the huddle of males, the females trumpet their arrival. Males shuffle to meet their partners with newly-hatched chicks on their feet.

Once the chicks are safely moved to females' feet, males can stretch for the first time in months.

September

For about fifty days, a chick sits on the feet of one of its parents, while the other parent goes to the open sea to catch food. When the foraging parent returns it will take over caring for the chick.

To get fed, chicks whistle and wave their heads up and down. The parent regurgitates food directly into the chick's mouth.

October–November

For the next few months, chicks are left at the colony while parents look for food. Moms and dads will return to feed their chicks as often as they can.

When it gets very cold, the chicks will huddle together to keep warm.

November

The colony is a very busy place in November. Parents are constantly coming to feed their chicks, then resting before going back out to sea to search for more food. Chicks are growing fast and are beginning to explore their world.

Chicks need big, elastic stomachs so they can quickly take in all the food their parents deliver.

December

In December the chicks molt, revealing a waterproof coat of adult feathers. As the ice breaks up, chicks leave the colony and head out to sea. Once their chicks leave, adults can feed and fatten themselves to prepare for their own molt which takes place in January.

The chicks' down is great for wind protection but will not keep them warm if they get wet. Before chicks grow their adult feathers, they need to stay out of the water.

Fact Files

Emperors of the Ice (*Aptenodytes forsteri*)

Emperors maintain a body temperature of around 100°F. Their feathers provide most of their insulation. The thick, scaly skin on their feet protects them from the cold of the ice. Blood pumped from the body warms the colder blood coming back from the feet, so the cold is not transferred to the rest of the body.

The Life Cycle

For the first six months of their lives, Emperor Penguins depend on their parents for food. Those that survive their first year will spend the next three years away from the colony. They begin returning at between three and five years of age. Their first attempts to breed and raise a chick often fail, but gradually, they will get it right. With their partner they try to raise one chick each year. Old age for an Emperor Penguin is 20 to 25 years.

Molting

Penguin feathers wear out and need to be replaced every year. For adults, changing of the feathers (the molt) occurs in January–February and takes about five weeks. New feathers are attached to the base of old feathers and push the old feathers out. Penguins need to eat a lot before this time because during the molt they don't eat, lose their insulation against the cold, and use energy to produce new feathers.

Fasting

Emperor Penguins have prolonged periods without eating (fasts) throughout the year. Adaptations like huddling, sleeping longer and eating snow to get moisture all aid energy conservation during fasts. Emperors also use fats for energy before they use muscle. There is more energy per ounce in fat than there is in muscle, and body weight drops more slowly as fat is consumed. When fat reserves become too low, the penguin must get food or it will starve.

Flying Underwater

Penguins are birds, like sparrows and chickens. They propel themselves underwater with strong beats of their wings. Penguins use their tail and feet as a rudder system. Their body has a perfect spindle shape to help reduce drag. Feathers across their body act in the same way as the holes in a golf-ball. They break surface tension and reduce friction during travel.

Prey

The Emperor Penguins' diet varies depending on what is available to them. In the Ross Sea area of Antarctica, Emperors mainly eat fish called Antarctic herring. Emperors in other parts of Antarctica may also eat Antarctic krill, Glacier squid, and other fish and squid species. Fish have a high fat content, so are the most nutritious prey for Emperor Penguins.

Swimming Records

Emperor Penguins hold the record for the deepest dive and longest breath-hold of any bird. The maximum depth recorded is 1850 ft, although only about 0.2 per cent of their dives go below 1300 ft. Most (70 per cent) are to depths shallower then 165 ft. The longest breath-hold, or dive duration, recorded for an Emperor Penguin is 21.8 minutes, although 95 per cent of dives last less than 6 minutes.

Predators

Emperor Penguins have two predators — Killer Whales and Leopard Seals. These predators often ambush the penguins as they enter or leave the water. Large numbers of penguins may gather at the ice edge, hesitating to enter in case a predator is there. Once one penguin jumps in, many others will follow. The burst of speed causes air trapped under the feathers to spurt out in a stream of bubbles into the water, which can further confuse predators.

Fact Files

Feeding chicks

Fathers produce a fatty, milk-like throat (esophageal) secretion to feed newly-hatched chicks. Chicks weigh just 8 ounces when born. They need many small meals every day. When they are approaching fledging age and weigh about 30 pounds, they can eat 8 pounds of food or more in one go. To raise a chick to fledging age, parents need to supply it with about 220 pounds of food.

Relatives

Standing 3.5 ft tall and weighing up to 88 pounds, Emperor Penguins are the largest penguins alive. The closest living relative of the Emperors are the King Penguins, which live on sub-Antarctic islands. King Penguins are almost as tall as Emperors, but weigh about half as much. While male Emperors do all the incubation of eggs, Kings have three shifts, each about 20 days long. The males do the first and last shifts and the females do the middle shift.

Roger Kirkwood spent a year living with Emperor Penguins on the Mawson Coast of Antarctica. He has participated in numerous research trips to study penguins and seals. When not venturing south, Roger works as a marine biologist for the Phillip Island Penguin Parade in Victoria, Australia.

For more information go to:

Phillip Island Nature Parks:
www.penguins.org.au

Antarctic Connection:
www.antarcticconnection.com/antarctic/wildlife/penguins/emperor.shtml

The Emperor Penguin:
www.emperor-penguin.com/emperor.html

Antarctic activities for schools:
www.classroom.antarctica.gov.au